# The Day The Bull Lived

And Other Poems

## BY
## CHRIS HEMINGWAY

11/8/25

To ~~[scribbled]~~

Enjoy the book!

Chris Hemingway

For Mom.

Forever in our hearts 5/31/2016

Mom. Thank you for always being there for me. I miss you every day.

Every rainbow I see. Every cloud in the sky.

I know that you are watching from above.

The Coming Spring

A Dream Is Like

Lamenting Of An Old Widow

The Dream Chaser

The Hope That We Desire

Midnight with Spanish Vermouth

Where Memories Have Gone

The Ashes Between the Daffodils

The View Over the Hill

The Bear

Silence in the Sun

Begotten Love Explained

The Empty Sun

As the Dawn Meets the Day

The Coming Drought

Angel, Beloved

Spring Intermezzo

Let me Sleep Once More

Though the Tomorrows Wonder

Where The Valleys May Go

Day Within a Day

Through The Heavens of Forever

The Ingredients in a Dream

Upon my heart's content

Overview

The last time I saw the Paris fireworks

Hemingway's Haiku

Through My Eyes Closed Blind

Of Remembrance Past

Intermission

Elysium Undefined

The Lullaby's Messenger

As The Rain Falls

Night Dream

Lament

Ode to the Wise

The Fortune Teller's Son

Night of the Falcon

The Candlemaker's Widow

The Loneliness of Winter

Love's Song

Upon The Floodwaters Door

Rumi's Lover

Conversation with the Moon

Live the Life

Ode to Papa

By the Shores of Cherry Creek Bay

The Fate of the Unknowns

The Holy Grail of Truth

Cherry Blossom Sunday

The Book Lover

Introspective

Night Stand

Ode to Papa-Part 2

Peace

Obsession

The Things We Once Called Love

Dream

Free Your Spirit

Poetry In Motion

The Girl with the Jack Kerouac Book

Bliss All Around

Ocean of Roses

For Notre Dame Cathedral.

The Day the Bull Lived

My best friend, Mom

The day the Bull Lived ©
Chris Hemingway has asserted his right under the Copyright, Designs and Patents Act 1988 to be identified as the author of this work.

ISBN: 9781689008846

No part of this book may be reproduced in any form or by any electronic or mechanical means including information storage and retrieval systems, without permission in writing from the publisher.
This book is a work of fiction. Names, characters, places, and incidents either are products of the author's imagination or are used fictitiously. Any resemblance to actual persons, living or dead, events, or locales is entirely coincidental.

For further information, contact the author at
chris_hemingway2003@yahoo.com

# The Coming Spring

Out of the cold of the winter there will emerge the beginning of spring. The flowers on the tree will grow once again and they are good flowers, ones that will welcome the choirs of life that seek its solace in the crisp air of the season that will soon begin.

On the eve of spring day, a solitary Robin emerged from the tree. And then another Robin came as he approached a flower and he saw that it was a strong flower one that can tempt the mighty oaks and battle the horde of locusts that approach en masse.

While this was happening, an assortment of butterflies joined in the fray and they saw the Robin on the flower and the armies of bees approaching, and the butterflies dismayed by all that was going on , sounded their call to the ants who came and followed and marched.

And the ants saw more Robins flying overhead, and the butterflies dancing around the daffodils while they looked at the bees pollenating and peered at the grasshoppers in the meadow and they looked for a way to build their mighty castles on the hills as they began to edge slowly toward the open pasture to their new home.

# A Dream Is Like

Stopping life for a moment
to gaze upon the longing road
of the silent shepherd
Wandering in a field of haze
to love the flower of the pale ghost
that is faded over a blue valentine
Longing forever in an eternal heartbeat
to stare at the rushing waterfall
swept by the tapering wind
Seeing light into darkness
to find a candle lit shadow
not lost in spirit but found in fate

# Lamenting Of An Old Widow

This life, a life of ashes, a life of daffodils, a life of shadows wrestling only mortal death pulled from the great barrier of life's lessons once unlearned, now forgotten into the stillness between the ocean depths that repent their grief-stricken tales of treeless dreams
the heart of understanding farewell and the rhythm of life tucked inevitably-free of blushing smiles, lacking form,
lingering indigent silence, imitation dream-lands, serenaded by the concrete spirits of the sanguine cold , an unrelenting moon who stands beneficiary of an unforgiving kingdom
admiring distant evening stars, a chorus of ravens by the harbor bridges lends mocking shrills and, cruelty to the solitary man in the iron boat washed ashore by chance
in the distance ahead, the lights motionless to eternity, fleeing the barefoot struggle draped in a cloudy fog
through these moments, there is hope, there is infinity, there is life once again until it is no more. only repose and confinement await,
the old widow sleeps, adheres to the ferryman and dreams of the light that burns once more

# The Dream Chaser

I see the dark shadow people, but I am paralyzed
Unable to grasp the blackness
Unwilling to fight the demons
Perchancing the unmendable heart
Realizing the remarkableness of fate unbeknownst
Seizing the times that feel so real but are unshaken dragons
Marching to the things that are not seen but are left frozen
Meditating familiar destinies that await but are delayed
I see the light ahead and it gives me cause
Able to break the chain
Willing to slay the inner beast of happenstance
Spurring the spirit of desire yet unbroken
Slaying the absence of pain fearlessly
Taking the dreams that are within reach but chaseable
Finally focusing on what needs to be dreamed
There is another rainbow-filled sky and another unbeaten path
There is the Frost-road of yore and the Byron-limericked tale
There are the folding skies of Tolkien that are waiting to be flown
There must be the golden land where the palaces are high and low
Dreams live on

# The Hope That We Desire

Bewildered within, impelled with repose
If the bells of the crier bled feelings
Where would the lonely day find solace in the teardrop-stained clouds?
Anger twisted, lies without form
If the rhymes of the saints penned truth
Why does the world breed hate?
Entranced disdain, flowers replace longing
If the soul can repent its hatefulness
Is there hope behind the veiled light?

# Midnight with Spanish Vermouth

Sitting in the summer chair
Fire and ice fill the air
Shadows and desire
Greet
Pain and love
Lament
Present and future
Laugh
Reflection and contempt
Eat
Put away the drink
Time to swallow life
Throw away the past
Future wants to breathe
No more wallowing
Searching for one last memory
Putting on boxing gloves
Throwing a punch at fate

# Where Memories Have Gone

Into the valley of that which has no name
Lies an abyss where moonlight stays still
Sunlight is a mystery; the rippling waves dance
Descending water-plants brush off the prowling morning dew
Upon the motionless, white depths, there lies a glimmer of life
It stirs the canal-deep forge, prancing the ocean-filled undertows
For a moment, a hope, a breath takes form only to be shuttered
By the luminary lights that have flickered away en masse
As the fairy queen sings her melodious tune of praise for the night
A solitary trumpet is heard by the congregation
All the angers and pains of the moments of the past are gone
A single glimmer of hope remains followed by silence
The night is no longer and the day is once more
In the end, all there is, is no more

# The Ashes Between the Daffodils

Beneath the continuous waves
of fire-still rainbows echoing silence
I came across a small copse of ash trees
Beside the billowing solitude of a honey-glazed oak
It's mighty gaze transfixed on his
His roots his torches; his leaves his embassies
Branching out to his purpose of the day
With every wind that blows, fortitude beckons
From every treetop in the valley, hope burns
On every summit peak, truth lives
Death and life desire time and patience

# The View Over the Hill

Watching

The candle dimming

The clock struggling

The hours crying

Time whispering

Remembering

Life happened

Hope championed

Truth mattered

Tears wiped

Wishing

For forever to be free

For our hearts to be enlightened

For our fates to be delivered

Humanity

Sits in stillness

# The Bear

Upon the old master about his business
over the fireside embers
with a white-grape fish hooked in his mouth
Vanity draws his rectitude
Seeing ferocious cauldron-like eyes
his prey hangs in chilling silence
Flinging its soul like a broken lyre
Trembling knowledge, praying for moonless nights
Cursing on his weed-stemmed rainbow
And inspecting his lowly abode
Half-loathing, quelling the passion
Frail-haunted and birthing death
He returns to the reverence of his frailty
And sleeps once more

# Silence in the Sun

Forget that sunflower that got mad as a fragment of love
Shutter the horizon which capitulated with dawn
Eyes open with dark wonder
Where worlds are like serpents
That glitter jeweled lips under the night
Lightning like fingers, casting our fears abay
Stars splash words, faltering with no fear
Objects concealed inside void butterflies
Be that new world, discovering gold hills and sounds
Hopeless dreams need not echo suffering's might
Create the colors of songs that dance without hearing the tune
And stand up and shout
To be heard once more

# Begotten Love Explained

The definition of love is like a birth of impossibility
Fate so truly parallels through infinite decrees
It merges two truths in one through perfect conjunction
It is not a blood oath taken by fate over the undershire
Nor is it a tyrranic despot who hands out roses to the rainbow he chooses
It is not the earth and the moon obliquely greeting each other at a magnanimous angle
It is simply like the wind blowing the daffodils in a row
It takes time and a nurturing patience like a seed planted by a dutiful gardner
It is the mingling of winds over Heaven and stone
It takes not what It receives, but gives when it is granted
Love knows only what it wishes and what is expected through time
In every shape or form, the bond of love is forever molded by choice in state
And by those who grace its presence and being
Love will always remain the hope of the spirit in waiting

# The Empty Sun

Digging the wasteland, there is another death that robs
I am shut out of hidden love
The long days of sweet madness
Here, waiting, my empty heart robbed of bridal laughter
For idleness is a thing that resides in agonizing reason
I wait in the narrow golden air in the absence of passion's sullen spring
Out of the remains of the beautiful undying road behind me
There lays a shadow of broken glass shards
I attempt to pick up the pieces
And remember
Of the love apart from us all

# As the Dawn Meets the Day

Rise to tender hearts over the mists at bay
Follow the lucid dreams as the morning unlearns
Illusions beckon speaking to the wild stallion in the cave
Speaking Centaurs, as the fire burns
Graying shadows lend credence to the watching willows at dusk
Spirit the fanning drone as the day reaches near
Wandering soul of the sky meant for the truest secret in the heart
No fate higher, as the moon stares
Secret sun hides truth behind light
Seering streamless starlight, trillowing beamless universe-like rays
Fantasies bane in the water of sanctity in the fall
The day is anew, as the dawn brushes her hair

# The Coming Drought

Under the veiled tree, I ponder life's trials and shames
Years of torment, hundreds of games
The times we mistake truth for happenstance under the shadows
Life, within a life; all but Shakespeare's tarried throws
A mere testament to the follies of truth and beauty
Her tightened bow in an age filled with ignorant courage and duty
Fear keeps growing within a dark secret like a foal from birth
Peaceful as a fire, most stern in the fields of molten earth
Nobleness is not natural, but high, solitary, apart from wonder
What is life? What abysmal fruits does it breed? Torn, broken amply asunder?
Do we follow its tracks in the sand, unshaken, unlearned?
Or lead a 1000 horses to the lonely charge, unfettered, unburned?
Dare, I not think of any more of life's lessons tonight
Rather, I follow the sinner in a gown of white

# Angel, Beloved

Broken eyes like teardrops with wings
Take thee into your hands
And make my traveled hands dance anew
Pray, angel beloved
Tearful goodbyes like torn thunder with serpents
Take my wanted wear into your divine ocean
And cleanse the soul of its shortcomings
Heal, angel beloved
Mountain sky like unending story with butterflies
Take my spirit and lift it to its woven clasp
And flood its gates with glittering sunflowers
Mercy, angel beloved
Hidden canyon like unfound temple with rubies
Take my unshackled coils from its lonely shell
And delight to liberate the mind of its confusion
Peace, angel beloved
Unspeckled rainbows like falling stars with memories
Take my hand and show me the open road
And teach me to follow the light
Fly, angel beloved

# Spring Intermezzo

Hades days of visionless horizons flown away
As darkness fights the night, winter is vanquished
The dusk alone glows heart's desire
Hopeless suffering no more
No more fire, no more toil, Mournful happiness ensues with Gaia
Coldness, blackness, a pale memory of old, Praying amongst the kindred
For light will set the music's interludes, beauty bestowed upon flower's dreams
Apollo-lyred minaturettes playfully mirror in sync with the wind, tenderlessly
Fitful-solitude elation succumbs in the clouds
As lilies frolic to brim an overture in the thunder's rain
Divine canaries bask in the golden lair, after day's end pluming
With eternal tender-swoon eyes, unchangeable splendor has regained her throne
Fragmented Elysium-filled waters mercilessly dance
Playing that which is not fit to be entertained
Feel Spring dance, reposed stars in hillside waltzes
Mistress-fashioned daisies stand close with the accepting wind
As sunset becomes acquainted with the night once more
Spring lays her laurel upon the breadth below

# Let me Sleep Once More

Introspective wheels measure the sun in my heart
Where mountains dare to sing, I cannot live without your porcelain smile
I cannot wander with the poor ghost anymore
I only want life to be fine, and without that empty letter
To harness lovely memories near the schoolhouse door
I defer my dreams, unto the meadow near the farmhouse
I charge, then I'm free, free to live without quaint, homesick eyes
Peering out my darkest ends
I am glad the empty letter is on the table
I won't read it, until I die for love
There is no reason why the shell of death haunts my innards
Or why it stumps my mistakes or daunts my honor
But this I know,
Nothing, every nothing
Bears fruit once more

# Though the Tomorrows Wonder

Tragedy of Betrayal, eludes the befuddled
Take not which we are granted, eluding withheld
Yet toil in the sanctity of hope, unmasked
O'er the fields of May, April blossoms die
Comedy of Truth, precedes our wisdom
Fight the uphill war of ignorance
With but a smile and a praise, though pale wonder
Into the canyon of desire, the mountains of fate wither
Spring of Torments, yields its beginnings
Ponder the destiny of a thousand wind-chimes in the snow
In a wink of a shadow, create the illusion that awaits
Burgeoning depths of hunger, the future longs for its purpose

# Where The Valleys May Go

Uncharted territory we reluctantly, merrily, tread
To discover the unburied secrets, happily as they lie
Into the beckoning depths we are forced, led
Where amber fruits settled upon most high
Where the valley leads are born the kingdoms, horizons, trees
Seven centuries once gone, fruitless vines, legends foretold
Still, onward we travel with tarried, harmless seeds
Where follies plague our mind, bolstered, mindfully behold
Look back we dare not say though penniless and frayed
Journeys hidden, souls cast upon the shore
Memories stolen, treasures spent, gaze upon the lurid wade
All we can want is to travel the maze once more

# Day Within a Day

Ghastly voices in the hall
Take my whims before I fall
Chant the limerick wrote for Byron
Dawnlight pretty falling siren
Whisper softly into deep
Follow slowly bring to keep
In the end for all to see
Daytime sweet I owe to thee
Into darkness holler, waver
Pale moonlight sunken, labor
Chain desire to the masts
Nighttime dark like drifting rafts
Mirror the day, quiet, weeping
Carpe diem flowing, seeping
Sic the bull until he runs
Day is over but undone

# Through The Heavens of Forever

The heart-colored roses waltzing by
A wind-shaped catamaran gliding down the omniscient-pearly shore
For a half-moment, peerlessly gaze overlooking the silver-lining-pendulum
Endlessly Dream not only a starry-eyed dream
But a prevalent timeless merry-go-round of fallacious chimes
Take a seat to graciously dine with the Four Emperors
Stargaze at the gold-rimmed fallen thrones
Snow-filled crowns like every-present harmonies
Dance endlessly into the seemlessly-unstarrry night
That silently awoke the tide-driven waves
Making the Poseidon-flowered sirens hopelessly astray

# The Ingredients in a Dream

What are dreams made of?

I think it is this

Sprinkle a little fairy dust

Not too much

Add a touch of imagination

Just enough

Pour a spoonful magic

To make it blend

Stir in some colors

Making it bubble

Simmer for 7 hours

When ready

Fly

When finished

Repeat

# Upon my heart's content

There is no time when a man can say
That his heart is neither loved nor despised
What grows on it is life
Life
The stuff that things are made of
It festers and wastes away the foundation of happiness
sometimes
We live
We die
As one
What more does the heart want
To be loved
To be shunned
Neither
We want the value of just being
To live the day
To see the light
Not to be judged or ignored
But to have the lasting precious time
Of being here

# Overview

Watching

The candle dimming

The clock struggling

The hours crying

Time whispering

Remembering

Life happened

Hope championed

Truth mattered

Wishing

Our future

terrorism-free

Our Earth

ignorance-free

Our hearts

Hate-free

Humanity

Sits in stillness

# The last time I saw the Paris fireworks

Upon the windswept hands that flow to thee
Feeling the charmed embraces of the same
Melancholy white sands along the hidden shore
Van Gogh's whispers I hear in my sleep
Where is my pretty one?
Is she sleeping at the night's pleasure?
Or taken aback by the storm
From whence the shadows pass, does please the same
Where do I go to see the Paris fireworks?
Is it raining daffodils?
Or has the wind danced on my soul?
Picasso's laughter in my dreams
Take me over the bridge of flames
Don't tell me I'm mad or insane
Or taken aback by the wheel of desires and shames
Lie to me, make me feel normal
And I'll do the same

# Hemingway's Haiku

Freedom lives
in our heart when we are trapped
Binding us

# Through My Eyes Closed Blind

I see a land filled with wonder
Yet there is danger
I peer though my sullen eyes
And see grayness
The green pastures marred with ashes
The rainbow too high to climb
In this world of chaos and mayhem
We must look past the ill-fated cynicism and bleak-filled clouds
Without the light of truth and patience
There is darkness that destroys
Hope that evades
Senselessness out of naught
Fantasy without imagination
Yet
When we open our eyes slowly
We change the heart of reality
Out of blackness, there is fortitude
In the air, breathes mysticism
Over the horizon, thrown luck
Through the valley, runs hope
I put on my new glasses
And see
Fate becoming one again

# Of Remembrance Past

Beauty is not natural
When it is fraught with blame
Stop life within a dream
On a starry, snowy evening
I carry no second dream
The moon and souls as witnesses


With courage that is solitary
Old Paris fills my days,
Walking tightened little streets
Peaceful, quaint as fire
Still, like Hector's Troy

Helen's porcelain  gaze blinds me

I cannot live wandering like a pale ghost
Clouded by starlights within my heart
The world and the moon collide
Charging like a bandless rage
Be glad that life is fine
And that the poor souls roam free

Why should misery hurl ignorant nobleness?

Listen and the truth be saved

# Intermission

Life is paused

Remember how the clouds looked

Or if the honeybee has made it to its destination.

Although the earth and sun greet

Do you see them play?

Stillness

The sounds of the world are dimmed

Only the sunshine between reality and fantasy remain

The rainbows dance

The melodies play

Yet in the quietude in the air

There is

Laughter

# Elysium Undefined

To go where the mighty horses stray

Beyond the gates of destiny and the streams of Tedium

In search of the ancient treasure beyond the blue pastures of Apathy

Where golden statues of Cronus line the formal parterre gardens

Lost, shipwrecked on the western edge of the Earth by the stream of Okeanos

Searching for the giant maze told by Pindar

Tell me, Rhadamanthus--Where do lilies lay?

Near the White Isle?

Or the far off motiff off Dilmun?

Where shall the journey commence?

Up the magic hills of Mount Teide

Over snow-capped volcano to Tenerife

Through the blessed garlands that make men weak.

Simple luxuries, intermittent showers, moist breezes, nourishing soils

Gently, settle the tides in the bay

And so the wind still waits

For its master to show

# The Lullaby's Messenger

Sing of the night that plays men's souls
To merry willows lay still in the darkness
The messenger of hope appears out of the wayward stillness
She dances a tune of slumbering ladybugs in the mist
Her shadows peer near but darkness eludes
Mighty wings chase to the mountain and are gone
Softly not do they sing their praise
But with pouring hope and mournful doubt
They rise again to be heard
Never-ending dreams of passing flutes pay its souls
Reality is not what it seems
But what dreams it shows

# As The Rain Falls

As the darkness appears

There is

Hatred

Ignorance

Despair

As the clouds form

There is

Doubt

Insincerity

Anguish

As the downpour begins

There is

Destruction

Flooding

Pain

As the fog lifts

There is

Bleakness

Dangers

Hope

As the sun shines

There is

Peace

Remorse

Understanding
As the day breaks
There is
Reckoning

# Night Dream

Chasing the butterflies over yonder!
While I weep and simply ponder!
Staring at the clouds, I merely wander!
Over the hills and through the brush!
Fast and daring--trying not to rush!
Falling and tumbling, down the creek below
A secret kingdom--so magical! so deep! I stroll!
Miniature unicorns! Tiny drum majors! -- I see!
Wondrous! Dancing! They hand me a key!
"Open the door!" They tell me, they sing! they play!
"It will lead you to your dreams," they say-
Saying goodbye, I approach the door made of oak!
Suddenly, I turn, I open, I'm awoke!
In my bed, I lay awake, still-dreams in my eye!
Asking, where oh where are the little people? I sigh!
As I turn, to go back to sleep, I stare!
Next to the nightstand, A golden key is here!

# Lament

Of the torture that frees
And the love that decays
There is blackness among forests
That prey on the locusts
Wallow
In the hidden people love scoffed
Left your thanks at the British bake off
Cover and uncover your mind
Untold treasures await behind
Rejoice
In the merry remains that lay
A shimmer of hope upon the bay
That shines upon the heavens above
In the form of white dove
Pray
That the sickening forevers tell
Of a rock strewn well
That no one can see
Except you and me

# Ode to the Wise

Hear these words sullen flower
That your bloom will rise aflutter
Speak not forever see you must
Upon laughter the seas will shutter
Remember this young fool
That dreams are not forgotten
To ends they will mostly see
And lives surely might have been
Shutter at the thought, tomorrow
In fields of bliss ye may
Seek to fight the higher bane
Only light will shine the way
Think before you listen
Let your emotions betray you not
From what slumbers may appear
Where others might forgot
Do not what others say
But merely follow your heart
For in the end we may parlay
To greener pastures we part

# The Fortune Teller's Son

Tell me oh great father of praise
Why do you know the things you do?
Is it because you want faith and fun?
Or do you want fables mistaken for none?
For nine years I traveled with you
I've seen the pyramids of old
Heard tales of the yogi's journey
And planted my thoughts with the monks at Llasa
But I have never seen
A smile on your face
Where mercies pain
And the lions sleep
I dream of the days
Where slumber reigned
And hopes bathed in the sun
Are we to go again
Where mythic explorers fade?
To hear of the silent ones
Where sleep is no more
Tell me captain of our ship
Why do you long for the maze?
It is because the journey means
There is one more story to hear
Or tredding spirits on the fields of glory

Don't make me a willing prisoner of your feat

All I want is

For you to read me a story

# Night of the Falcon

Like the mighty roar
Seven sails to the shore
Where eagles dream, the memories stream
The falcon greets the day once more
Into unchartered flight
Within distant sight
Let the chase begin, the strong shall win
He begins his quest until dusk
Amid whine and circumstance
His talon, his lance
Forcing nature on the lam, the wind be damned
He fights the good battle, lost and won
Just one more journey
To make his hurry
Bleeding strength through honor, the fates cry yonder
The night belongs to him
As the night grows near
He chases his stare
Soaring back to home, the day's alone
He rests, thinking of tomorrow in the sun

# The Candlemaker's Widow

She sleeps as though she is awake

Twenty years past

Alone

Tired

Hungry

Unable to move

Unable to think

Trying to catch one last breath

She cries as though she is happy

Ten summers past

Afraid

Doubtful

Hopeful

Unwilling to fight

Unwilling to yield

Forcing herself to move on

She laughs as though she is fearless

Present day

Unmoving

Unshaking

Indisposable

Anxious for the day to come

Anxious for the night to begin

# The Loneliness of Winter

Winter

Is

Nuances

Threads

Everyday

Remorse

In

Silence

# Love's Song

Hearts ablaze
Torn asunder
Rippling waves
Roaring thunder
Tides engulfed
Mountains weep
Forever eternity
Falling deep
Night's embrace
Raging mire
Deaths slumber
Passion's fire
Heavens abound
Destinies await
Hope's glory
Mercy's fate

# Upon The Floodwaters Door

Through pain and sorrow

We mourn for those who have suffered at the hands of mother nature

Through tears and humility

We thank the ones who risk their lives to save us

The rivers have overflowed their banks

But cannot flood our soul

The fires can burn our homes

But cannot extinguish our spirit

We fight against the elements

Because we have the will to do so

We strive to rebuild

Because we have the strength that guides us

In the end

In this eternal battle with the elements

We go on

Until the sun rises again

# Rumi's Lover

Go rest your tired head on your beaten pillow
Shake off your sleep with a whisper
Don't talk don't speak
Just listen
To the sounds of the cold winds
That pound against the window of your soul
Dream but a dream
About your fortunes told
Tender your spirit to unfettered blessings
Reading between minds that seek to
To lasting purity that binds the frays of attachment
To love that lasts
To love that fails

# Conversation with the Moon

I saw the moon one night

He was laughing at me

I asked him

Why do you torment me with your smile

He said

There is one thing you haven't done in your life and cant do

I said

I have traveled the seven seas and found vast treasures

I am the richest person and have many kingdoms

I can do anything I want

The moon smiled and said

Have you put hope in a jar

The moon smiled again at me

# Live the Life

The winds of change are upon us
Do we not dare where it will take us
or if let alone succumb to its will
but if we are swept by the wind
we must simply
glide

# Ode to Papa

You charmed us with your words, your smile, and your life
You were a man's man, a writer's writer, and a symbol of bravery that most people look for in 20 lifetimes and still look for
You chased the bulls, fished the mighty seas, and looked at fear and simply winked at it
You traveled the world, reported the wars, and braved death and leapt over it
You were taken from the world too soon.
You still capture the imagination, shape our words, and force us to imagine big.
You continue to inspire us to chase the marlin, defeat the odds, and overcome adversity and be on top.
You whisper to us to be alive, brave the fight, and rise to the occasion
You will always be the World's Papa.

# By the Shores of Cherry Creek Bay

Not far from the old abandoned lighthouse
and past a stone's throw from the old wooden mill
I made a summer's vow
The wind was my inspiration, the pebbles my audience, the
waters my witness
I pledged to live the life I would choose
to gather the worth and dignity of everything i stand for
and to muster up the courage I could find to believe in the light
With that vow said. It began to thunderstorm
I ran off under a tree to seek solace.
Were the fates listening? I do not know
What's important is this:
Bring an umbrella for life's obstacles

# The Fate of the Unknowns

There was a time when we seek to
Help someone or something that always
Ends in
Failure. We do not
Attempt to fail or nor do we
Try to fail in our
Efforts
Over the years if we do
Fail it is not in our vocabulary or in our
Tired little head either.
Herein lies the question of my prologue to you:
Ever tempt the
Unknown?
No one has to date and lived to tell about it.
Kindred spirits lock heads like
No spirit known.
Only can
We know the unknown can we harness its power
No one can know the fate of the unknowns
So life goes on

# The Holy Grail of Truth

Here is a truth that I know
Of. It
Lies deep within
You. It is the essence of your
Goals and the far
Reaches of your mind
And
It
Lies not
Only in the
Fortune that you create but also it
Trancends the
Riches that you want. It is
Underneath all of your emotion and
Tries to come out once and a while but is
Hidden.
Find your holy grail.
It lies in you.

# Cherry Blossom Sunday

Chasing a kite that was taken captive by the wind one Sunday, I
Happened to come across a delightful tree. I looked at her
Endlessly. She was
Riveting and
Remarkable. It was as if I discovered a new language.
Year after year I would visit this
Bountiful tree. I would
Lounge under her shade and
Over her protection.
She was a
Sanctuary that
Only I knew of. She
Made me cry and laugh and
Sing. As the years went on I went
Under her shade one more time. I always say
Nothing ever
Dies unless you want it to
Always will I remember that fateful day I saw her when I was
Young.
I will always be under the cherry blossom tree

# The Book Lover

Tedious

He reads

Endlessly

Behind his

Owly eyes he

Opens the doorway to another dimension

Keeping his secret book where it

Lays dormant in an unused box

Over the desk he

Veers off into an

Endless array of

Reading

# Introspective

Truth is the only thing that lives
With every breath the earth takes
becomes a wallowing divergence
to what all the doomed days may occur
only hope lives unto the end

# Night Stand

Softly the echoes
Dance into the night gently
Suddenly chimes ring
The writer sits down
At his desk slowly writing
Loneliness awaits

# Ode to Papa-Part 2

Writing is bleeding the great writer said
The writer writes
Day after day
Night after night
Striving to put good in existence
Or to place bad where it shouldn't be
Writing is bleeding alright
When we bleed, do we not feel the pain?

# Peace

It is the instrument
that plays a song
that no one can hear
but if you listen carefully
you can hear it
not everyone can hear it
but those who hear it
are changed forever

# Obsession

I danced with the Queen of Hearts
and got into a fight with the King of Clubs
The Jack of Diamonds bought me in a drink
I told the Queen of Diamonds that she looked pretty
and the Ace of Spades wants to hang out with me next Friday
night. I'll ask the Jack of Spades to buy me another drink and I
think the Queen of Clubs gets off work at 9. The Queen of
Spades and the Jack of Hearts are out tonight while the King of
Spades stays home. I want to be like the King of Diamonds.

# The Things We Once Called Love

That late night dinner you used to make
The diner where you dropped the plate
The bed where we lied awake
The parking lot where you would make me wait
Sing me a tale of your song
Write me a poem and tell me your wrong
I shutter to think of the lies you once told me yesterday
In the end it doesn't matter its over and away
One final piece I liked for you to see
Is the way we used to seem to be
Was is real was it lie
Sometimes I'm wide awake and say why

# Dream

Pull down your hair,
Let the wind in your face,
Only you hold the key to your dreams,
Dream a little dream
Dream until there are no tomorrows,
Dream until the oceans run dry
Dream until the rainbows fade
Until the last moment your dream becomes real
Dream until the realities become dreams
And there is nothing left to dream about...

# Free Your Spirit

Go hither and
Release your
Energy then travel
Enter a realm
Nobody but you
Over the horizon
Listen to your echo
Invite your senses
Open your mind
Empty your thoughts
See the light
Praise the heavens
Be the master
Follow your dream
Take the chances
Sound the trumpet
No one can do it
Except you

# Poetry In Motion

On a summer's day
Evervescent flowers
Twirling all the way
Reveling in the sunlight
Young lovers holding hands
In the Parisian streets
Strolling in the night
Laughter in the morning
Intertwined in love
Falling for
Enchanting signs from above
Neverending excitement
Explore the paintings of life
All around us
Always in motion

# The Girl with the Jack Kerouac Book

She's the girl with all the answers/she spends her day drinking whiskey with lemon/she puts in all in perspective/without delay/searching for the answers in the wrong places/but she doesn't stop at that doesn't know what she truly wants/except wants a new adventure every second/rolling with the punches/making every day seem like climbing a rollercoaster/wanting and wishing/to go home

# Bliss All Around

Young-picked tulips in a bow
Omniscient togetherness
Underneath the mistletoe
Aroma of rose colored petaldust in the air like
Refined pearl oyster beads singing
Enchanting waltzes of uncouthed magnitude
Memories that make canyons crave
Yellow-tailed butterflies in a row
Angelic glows of heavenly melodies
Nocturnal music flows in the mist-filled night as
Gentle breezes of summer days past create
Enthralling harmony
Love is all around

# Ocean of Roses

In my dreams you sing me

Lullabies dressed in little blue dresses filled with a bouquet

Of daisies and beautiful rainbow-colored

Violets wrapped in

Every time I think of

You I wonder of our future together and I dream of swimming in

an

Ocean filled with roses where we

Understand that

Sometimes dreams are

Oceans waiting to be swam. I swim in your

Pleasure, dance in your

Happiness. And I

Invite myself to your dreams where I simply

Enjoy the ocean of roses

Where I swim and

Can be free

# For Notre Dame Cathedral.
May you shine your light again for all to see
4/15/19

I see Paris crying yet what can I do
Her daughter is on fire, bleeding
Her brothers and sisters rush to aid, save
What can we do but watch and wait
I see Paris in pain yet how can I help
Her torch touches the heavens, mountains
Her hands rise up to soar like eagles, doves
What does the heart tell us to believe
I see Notre Dame in flames
Her spire fallen but not forgotten, unshaken
Her spirit fractured yet intact, unwavering
What magics lay ahead in the city of dreams
I see the Parisian people by the carousels
Their hearts lifted, consoled
Their minds filled, made whole
I see the Paris fireworks dance again

# The Day the Bull Lived

They say the ghosts of the bulls charge in Pamplona. The pale whispers of their mighty roars can be heard as the wind blows in the distance. They cry for their fallen brothers in anguish and in mourning of the night before the bullfight, before the death in the afternoon. An unrelenting moon stands beneficiary of an unforgiving kingdom, admiring distant evening stars. A chorus of vultures by the harbor bridge lend mocking shrills and cruelty to the solitary man in the iron boat. In the distance ahead, the lights flash motionless to eternity, fleeing the barefoot struggle, draped in a cloudy fog. Tomorrow is the day of reckoning.

A solitary raven emerged from the tree. And then another one came as he approached a flower and he saw that it was a strong flower one that can tempt the mighty fates and battle the horde of locusts that approached en masse. While this was happening, an assortment of butterflies joined in the fray and they saw the crow on the flower and the armies of bees approaching, and the butterflies dismayed by all that was going on, sounded their call to the ants who came and followed and marched. and the ants saw more ravens flying overhead, and the butterflies dancing around the daffodils while they looked at the bees pollinating and peered at the grasshoppers in the meadow and they looked for a way to build their mighty castles on the hills.

As they began to edge slowly toward the open field, the bull slept like a lamb out of heaven. He awoke and yawned like a lion and admired the view over the hill. Watching the candle dimming, the clock struggling, the hours crying, and time whispering, he remembered how life happened, truth reigned, and tears mattered. He began wishing for forever to be free, for hearts to be enlightened, and for fates to be delivered. Under the veiled tree of life's trials and shames, lay years of torment, hundreds of games, and blood upon the sand. Today, one more spectacle ensues, one more death match poison, and one more memory flows into the abyss.

People began to fill the arena like tiny drum majors, marching to the things that are not seen but are left frozen. Bringing gifts from far away, the thorn-less roses shine redness upon the arena while the cheers echo until eternity. As the crowd fills, there emerges a sudden stillness. The sounds of the world are dimmed and only the sunshine between reality and fantasy remain. As the rainbows dance and the children play there is quietude in the air yet laughter dances its way on stage as the entourage makes its way to the grandstand.

Leading the way dressed in his Philip II costume, the alguacil gives his marching orders to the matador. The picadors chuckle and prance as the sword handlers parade behind the congregation. The matador dons his black hat, drags his foreboding cape along the sand, and stammers his graceful, unreachable confidence. As peaceful as a fire, the bull marches slowly before his doom. He is followed by Death who is the last one to enter the arena. Wine-soaked toy soldiers taunt with the beast but the bull stands unafraid, unrelenting, and unsinkable to the wishes of the fear that is expected to encompass him. The game was about to begin.

The Ill-fated matador begins to tempt the bull hopelessly. Like an old master about his business, he rushes, lunges at his opponent. Into death's arms he lays to the gates of hell, he marches, the bull erupts like a spewing volcano. Alone, defeated, towering, the bull tires like a faint whisper. Death slowly peers from the crowd to stare his prey into oblivion and lay his laurel upon the breadth below.

Piercing, bold, determined, the bull forges ahead. He takes a jab, a puncture, a breath, throwing a punch at fate. A miss, a near miss, the bull dodges his enemy's blow running like a sinner in purgatory. Charging, roaring, running, the bull fights on amidst the jeers of the crowd's porcelain smiles.

Ole. Ole. Ole

The crowd cheered.

The bull ran like the wind. Like an unshaken freight train, huffing breaths of disgust and lament, the bull grew weary of the prolonged suffering at the hands of his elegant killer. Looking into his eyes, he sees the determination of his foe, the depths of the struggle, and the contrast to his own frail-haunted body. Numb determined, and focused, the bull stopped. He prays to his fallen brothers and to the archangel above.

"Angel, Beloved. Broken eyes like teardrops with wings, take thee into your hands and make my traveled feet dance anew.

Pray, angel beloved. Tearful goodbyes like torn thunder with lightning, take my wanted wear into your divine ocean and cleanse the soul of its shortcomings. Heal, angel beloved. Mountain sky like unending story with butterflies, take my spirit and lift it to its woven clasp and flood its gates with glittering sunflowers. Mercy, angel beloved. Hidden canyon like an unfound temple with rubies, take my unshackled coils from its lonely shell and delight to liberate the mind of its confusion. Peace, angel beloved. Unspeckled rainbows like falling stars with memories, take my hand and show me the open road and teach me to follow the light. Fly, angel beloved." He was ready to die. He was ready to bear his testimony and languish before the choirs of plenty.

But sometimes, courage and luck marry themselves upon us. A shimmer of hope plays fortune upon the bull. From the clouds above, a sign in the form of a white dove appears. Soaring like the mighty eagle, seven sails to the shore, the dove rests on the bull's forehead.

The crowd stares in wonderment by this unmistakable form of happenstance as if the bull is being ordained by the Holy See himself. Through these moments, there is hope, there is infinity, there is life once again.

He will live to dream. He will live to see another day. He will live to see the golden land where the palaces are high and low. There is another rainbow-filled sky and another unbeaten path and cloudless skies that are waiting to be flown, slaying the absence of pain fearlessly and taking the dreams that are not within reach but chaseable. The bull continued to stand majestic. The white dove then flew onto the matador, resting his tiny body on the brim of his hat, unwavering in his quest for a longing, lasting peace to unfold. Flinging its soul like a broken lyre, trembling knowledge and solace, praying for starry nights, the dove sings his melody to the masses. Cursing on his weed-stemmed rainbow and inspecting his lowly abode, the dove looks into the crowd, full of half-loathing creatures that are pure and robbed of innocence. Quelling passion, birthing freedom, and restoring sanctity, the dove anoints the bull with song and verse like a sounding harp. He then flew off into the sunset, returning to the humbleness of his solitude and on to its next mission of mercy.

The crowd cried, they wept, they toiled. Bewildered within, impelled with repose, as if the bells of the crier bled feelings. It was as if anger twisted itself upon its lies without form and somehow the rhymes of the saints penned truth in stone. The hope they somehow desired
buried deep within the layers of confinement were suddenly thrust upon the searing landscape. Entranced, washed of disdain, flowers replaced longing and the soul repented its hatefulness.

Live. Live. Live.

They chanted.

The bull was immediately escorted out of the ring, by his unwilling hosts. Bouquets of roses were thrown from the balconies as old women did the sign of the cross as he was led away.

He was brought to the corral, surrounded by his thoughts, and thinking about the events of the day. The bull came across a small copse of ash trees beside the comfort of a honey-glazed oak. Death and life desire time and patience, he thought. Luck took her place among the stars along with her soulmate, courage.

The bull then rested his head upon the grass, began to dream about the reverence of his frailty, and drifted to sleep once more.

# My best friend, Mom

People come and go in life
But there is always Mom
Though the mountains may fall and the stars fail to grant wishes
Mom takes up the torch
A thousand suns can't radiate
The warmth of a smile from Mom
When the world seems desperate
We turn to Mom
She is the first person who comes to help
She is the last person standing there in the end
When the darkness falls and hope seems at a loss
Mom becomes the lighthouse where the ocean ends
A beacon of truth and light
always searching for her lost ship at sea